Oxford University Press, Walton Street, Oxford OX2 6DP

*Oxford London Glasgow
New York Toronto Melbourne Auckland
Petaling Jaya Singapore Hong Kong Tokyo
Delhi Bombay Calcutta Madras Karachi
Nairobi Dar es Salaam Cape Town*

and associated companies in
Beirut Berlin Ibadan Mexico City Nicosia

OXFORD is a trade mark of Oxford University Press

First published in Germany by Verlag Heinrich Ellermann, Munich, 1986
Der rote Handschuh
© Verlag Heinrich Ellermann, Munich, 1986
© English version: Oxford University Press 1987

All rights reserved. No part of this publication may be reproduced, stored in a retrieval system, or transmitted, in any form, or by any means electronic, mechanical, photocopying, recording, or otherwise, without the prior permission of Oxford University Press.

This book is sold subject to the condition that it shall not, by way of trade or otherwise, be lent, re-sold, hired or otherwise circulated, without the publisher's prior consent in any form of binding or cover other than that in which it is published and without a similar condition including this condition being imposed on the subsequent purchaser.

The Red Mitten

Story by Tilde Michels
Illustrated by Winfried Opgenoorth

English version by Ron Heapy and David Fickling

Oxford

Who has lost this nice red mitten
for a little hand to fit in?
Lost among the leaves and flowers,
it could lie alone for hours.

Then a deer comes through the thicket,
sniffs it once and tries to lick it.
'That red mushroom looks a treat.
Might be crunchy. Might be sweet.'
Comes up nearer. Comes up closer.
One good sniff. Oh Deer, no, sir!
'Goodness me, I'm out of luck,
this is just a load of yuk.'
Lowers his antlers—and then woosh,
chucks it into the elder bush!

Hoppity-hop, here's Mother Hare,
sees it hanging over there.
'Who in the woods threw this away?
Waste not, want not's what I say.
This must be a hare's ear cosy,
will it fit on Fred or Rosie?'
Tries it on. 'It's much too small.
This little hat won't fit at all.
This isn't such a lucky find.
Off we hop and never mind.'
The little red mitten is left behind.

Spring has passed, then June, July—
look, here's a dancing butterfly.
Down it gently flies and flutters,
has a taste and then it mutters,
'From up there it looked like honey,
now I'm here it tastes real funny.'
But butterflies don't stay for long,
they dance away to the Summer song.

A raven spies it from on high,
and fixes it with his beady eye.
'Now what's that thing supposed to be?'
And he swoops down quick from his lofty tree
'Kra, Kra,' he croaks with a shrilly shriek,
'I don't like red!' Then with his beak
he takes it up and away he flies.
'Kra, Kra, Kreh, Kreh,' he cackles and cries.
'I'll fix this thing, make no mistake,
I'm going to drop it in the lake.'

Down drops the mitten without stopping,
lands in the water, wet and sopping.
Floats a while but soon will sink,
but here comes help—quick as a blink,
swimming fast across the lake,
a noisy duck and a hungry drake.

'It's mine!' says Drake 'You're out of luck.'
'I saw it first!' quacks angry Duck.
She pulls it this way, he pulls back,
the battle starts, 'Quack' answers 'Quack.'
The language starts to get quite rude,
until they see it isn't food.
Says Duck 'This isn't any use,
I think we ought to call a truce.'
And so as friends they swim to land,
and leave the mitten on the sand.

The mitten sees the Summer go,
the winds of Autumn start to blow.
The leaves are falling from the trees,
and very soon the lake will freeze.
The mitten knows it's truly lost,
once it feels the touch of frost.

Snow begins to fall at night,
the mitten now is snowy white.
All the ground is cold and bare,
snowflakes, snowflakes everywhere.

Winter passes, now it's Spring,
all the birds begin to sing.
One fine warm and sparkling day,
the snowy carpet melts away.
Suddenly the world is green,
and all the creatures can be seen.
There's the mitten in a pool,
feeling like an April fool.

The mitten feels it's useless now,
but then two birds upon a bough
see it lying on the ground,
'Just the thing.' 'Look what we've found.'
Says Mr to Mrs, 'Let me suggest,
we'll use that thing to pad our nest.'
Down they fly and then they start
to pull the soft red threads apart.

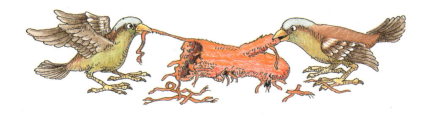

They build the nest with care and love,
it's warm and soft and like a glove!
Then Mrs lays one egg, then two,
and soon there will be lots to do.
A week or so and then they hatch,
upon the mitten's soft red thatch.
Warm and cosy the two chicks lie,
and they'll be safe until they fly.

First the mitten was dropped and lost,
then picked up by a deer and tossed.
Then became a hat for a hare,
plucked up by a raven, flown through the air.
Dropped in the water, pulled by a duck,
it seemed that the mitten would find no luck.
Now all the mitten's troubles have passed,
it's found a happy end at last.

That was one story about the little red mitten, but Tom can tell you another.
And this is how it begins: In a playground . . .

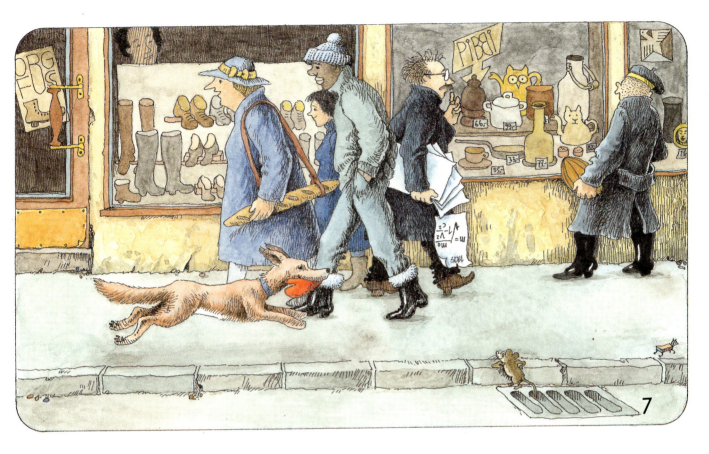

And how do you think this story should end?
Like this . . .?

Or like this . . .?